COLOR
PHOTOGRAPHS
OF THE RUINS

COLOR PHOTOGRAPHS OF THE RUINS

ELTON GLASER

University of Pittsburgh Press

Pittsburgh • London

The publication of this book is supported by grants from the National Endowment for the Arts in Washington, D.C., a Federal agency, and the Pennsylvania Council on the Arts.

Published by the University of Pittsburgh Press, Pittsburgh, Pa. 15260
Copyright © 1992, Elton Glaser
All rights reserved
Eurospan, London
Manufactured in the United States of America

Library of Congress Cataloging-in-Publication Data

Glaser, Elton.
    Color photographs of the ruins / Elton Glaser.
        p.   cm. — (Pitt poetry series)
    ISBN 0-8229-3705-0. — ISBN 0-8229-5468-0 (pbk.)
    I. Title. II. Series.
    PS3557.L314C6   1992
    811'.54—dc20   91-50758
                                                              CIP

A CIP catalogue record for this book is available from the British Library.

I am grateful to the following magazines, which have published or will soon publish many of the poems in this collection: *Abraxas* ("Traveling Sideshow: Corpse with Hair Growing"); *Art Academy News* ("A Late Theory of Reading"); *Chariton Review* ("Vacation" and "Orpheus at the Orpheum"); *Cincinnati Poetry Review* ("After Listening to the Only Tape of the March 1956 Reading in Berkeley," "Poem Written with the Eyes Closed," and "Proles Before Swans"); *Colorado Review* ("In the Offing"); *Fine Madness* ("Cheap Replicas of the Eiffel Tower," "Heliotropic," "Coup de Théâtre," "Far North of Ponchatoula," "Suicide by Marriage," and "Exploded View of the Universe"); *5 AM* ("Coroner"); *The Incliner* ("*Film Noir*"); *Indiana Review* ("Blues for the Nightowl"); *Laurel Review* ("Color Photographs of the Ruins" and "Sepulchritude"); *Memphis State Review* ("Ghost Excursion"); *New Virginia Review* ("Missing Mayakovsky"); *North Dakota Quarterly* ("Ditch Lilies"); *Ohio Journal* ("White Socks and Polkas"); *Pacific Review* ("Slow Classes at the Music School"); *Poetry* ("Confluences at San Francisco"); *Poetry Northwest* ("At the James Wright Poetry Festival," "A Riff for Isadora," "Elegy with Sideburns," "Insomniacs at the Feet of Science," and "Hymn and Harangue for Hesperus"); *Southern Humanities Review* ("Bible Browsing") and *Southern Poetry Review* ("Every Harmonica Player Needs a Train Song").

I would also like to thank the National Endowment for the Arts for a fellowship that helped make this book possible. And for advice that helped put this book back on track, I am especially grateful to my friend and colleague, Robert Pope.

in memory of
Raeburn Miller

for kindnesses too many to tell

Contents

COLOR
PHOTOGRAPHS
OF THE RUINS

Traveling Sideshow:
Corpse with Hair Growing

The barker's three-day beard
glistened like pitch in the downpour;
and half-hearing his spiel of hormones
beyond the law, beyond the spayed pages
of our schoolbooks, we gazed on
the garish panels of his van:
a dead woman naked in a box, her hair
pulsing beside her as if to taunt
the hands that had, while living,
bound it like bellropes. And we lined up,
clutching our quarters in the backstreet storm,
eyes eager for that long mane wild
between her thighs, fool's money
in the hunt for love out of hard weather.

Vacation

The avenues are open and swooping with palm trees.
It's Florida, home of the hot whistle and the sand dollar,
Cheap tours with the housewife-aviatrix.

We lounge on the long beaches and the lifeguards
Bark in their megaphones and oh god you've lost
Your ruby earring, the tides are smuggling it out to Cuba.

In back of the bedridden motel, the reptile gardens
Broadcast the gator's complaint, the sneer of the rattlesnake.
And consenting couples sink in their own sweat.

But at this altitude, the keys could just as well
Be the isles of Langerhans and the state
A wormy appendix preserved in a salt solution.

Over the fantasy of acres and ocean, we fly
By our shadow, snug in the greasy parachutes,
Dead calm at the eye of the triangle.

Every Harmonica Player Needs a Train Song

Back when the Seven Seas down St. Philip Street
Was the last bar messed up enough
To take you in—vagrant tables; Dixie tapped out—
And you would, on weekends,
Drive home drunk at dawn, your left wheels
Lame against the neutral grounds,
No radar, and the dashboard dialed in to Holy Rollers
Stumping the white folks for Jesus,
Or the lachrymose melancholia of cowgirls in hell,

You lived uneasy near the twin enigmas, hard by
The outskirts of women
And the closed borders of poetry. If you had straddled
The damage those days had done,
Or burrowed back down
The darker passages, like a coon in kudzu,
Would you now flinch awake
At the third mugging of coffee, and feel the past
Peel back, the years revealing
What all lines of love come down to?

Bible Browsing

and the Lord will discover their secret parts

—Isaiah 4:17

Taking the prophets at random,
I let my luck
find its own way on the page, as it did
those winter birthdays before
my adolescent oils and angst, when I would
spin the bottle and watch its glass mouth
slow and stop, always open to some girl
who frightened me, whose lips
my lips would kiss in the overcoated dark
of a closet, the door held hard against
sneers and pity in the listening room,
ten years old and yearning
to faint into the flesh, the secret
soundings of the tongue, as now
my heart shakes again, braving
the stern verse some fool from Jerusalem
drooled into his beard, a promise that
the world would press against us
like a hand against a desert honeycomb,
and let the six-sided riddles
drip their sweetness
down the cleft flanks of stone.

Seduced and Abandoned

Tired of the new austerities,
Thin season
Of farewells to the flesh,
He stares at the last stained copy
Remaindered from his classic text,
Postcoital Cuisine, and does not regret
The loss of that woman who
Steered him nightly to the bright rooms
Laid with sorghum and the raw panels
Of shark and papaya, her belly pulled back
By resistant machines, her mind
Bent on the raise and the raisins.

What can he do now but turn—
A free lance
Blunt and pointed low, not blood
But rust on the blade—
Turn back to his notes stricken with
The inarticulate twitch of the young,
Fragments hunched and abandoned, in need
Of a fusing hand, an eye dark enough
To build another damaged book,
Postmortal Decor, as if he could
Unearth from black plaques and emblemata
Some provisional perfection of the page,
The last word on last things.

Ghost Excursion

I've gone through the history of being human—
thighs spangled with sperm, dead men
sweetened to a high gloss as if they were
kittens on a calendar—
and arrived on the other side where
you wait, all lemons and piano lessons and laundry
coming clean in the dry air like Jesus.

It's true, I lived in the madness of gin
and christened my cock with strong oils, less holy
as the nights unbuckled into dawn, giving
no quarter to laws or money, loving only
what my lips could suck in or soothe away.
This is the face I built out of black birthdays.

Now you promise me a mattress to repent on,
the ticking fireproofed and the frame
screwed down, around me a ring of children
meant to witness and overcome
the old stains and dangers of the bed.

O you can bleach and scour, but it won't take.
I'll never open like that dogwood
unfolding its petals upright to the sun,
white clusters bleeding at the heart. Bring me
the poisoned rose of the oleander, a wand
to wave me out of here, the sequel
of flesh in a furious sleep, back to
the weeds and the boneless women,
back to the crimes I was born for.

Cheap Replicas of the Eiffel Tower

"Not altogether a fool," said G——, "but then he's a poet, which I take to be only one remove from a fool."

—Edgar Allan Poe

Nuclear ecstasy on the picket line;
Another homily on hominy; the lacquer of tears
Sealing in the wrath of wronged women—

Christ, I'd rather be
Crouched at the slick end of an alley
In the Costa del Sol Bowl-A-Rama and Cocktail Lounge,
Eyeing the 7–10 split,

Than stand up for these anthems
Of amnesia and the undefiled,
Recombinant aesthetics
Backed by the third degree; I'd rather

Hose down the sidewalks of Bourbon Street
After the fatback extravaganza,
Drizzly auditions for the freak parade,

Than plot odes against the birdbath,
Sestinas with the sneer of sequins, as if
I were born fairhaired in Toronto, a town
So dead no one spits on the asphalt.

Elsewhere, they're sweetening theories
For sheep and the French—I can feel
My brain back up with
Dry ironies, romance of the verb,
Those arbitrary accelerations
That flare as thought the great bang and spangle
Fused for the 4th of July
Had gone up some muddy midday in March.

Elsewhere, he's putting a new prong
On his pen, buffing an ego
Big as a beerwagon horse; and she,
Profile moist to the moon, has mistaken
The patois on the patios
For the dark spirals of praise. O let them
Spank the words with their tongues,
Until passion pours out
Smoke corrosive on the brain.

Still riddled by the heart's assignments,
The midnight secrets of the lips,
I want only to
Board the last bus to Parnassus,
Hoping there to take on
The torque and surefoot, the rank shag
Of the mountain goat, whose impervious gaze
Angles up the slant, scarp to white ledge:
Beauty once more mounted by the beast.

Suicide by Marriage

In love, the only victory is flight.
—Napoleon Bonaparte

The password for today is *Pussy under mink.*
Much better than last week, when you would open
Only to the penetrating cry
Épater les artistes. That's why I brought

This bullwhip and a box
Of bowtied roses, their perfume irretrievable,
Trailing you like a skulk of foxes,
The odor of lost lust—

Bodies spilt in the wrong rooms
When the hour was up and heaving.
One source of your folly is
Living this way while the world

Still looks for its shadow,
Like a sundial whacked with mud.
But these days everyone's a critic,
Kicking the tires, poking around

The innards of the enigma: snipers
Who twist the crosshairs to a slick fit
And neglect to dope in
The wind and the laws of gravity.

Why should I spend myself asking
How many pinheads can dance
On the pate of an angel,
When a few durable apologies would do?

—My choice to lie here hefting
The small potbelly of your breast,
Wondering into whose hands you will pass
When the timeclock springs its trap

And you go off, halfcocked,
To work and the ways of men;
Or to find myself clamped down
In the last damp row at midnight,

Eyeballing the voyeurs,
While the pink fleshfalls of film
Outflank and glaze
The homely and the homeless and the unsurprised.

Blues for the Nightowl

What must a man do in this house
to get a drink? Your birds back up
against the liquor cabinet, their goldtone cages
blocking the door. I don't want candy bottled
by Italian girls with their beads and depilatories,
or rare Shanghai decanters of three-penis wine.
Bring out the sweet mulekick of bourbon,
plummet and catapult of cheap gin. It's not so much
the thirst that bothers me, no dusty tongue,
but the long hole that empties into emptiness.
Take down that barricade of seedball peckerwits,
crack out the ice, the taxing seals, and let me
pour this life until it laps against the end.

Jabu Screaming

In the dark desert, among
The goats and the clanking tanks,
Jabu says:
The end of the world will come
After the headlines and the deadline,
Fumes and smears of the late edition.

And Jabu screaming, screaming
That God is Great.

There is sand in his scream,
The pock and polish of a throat
Open at full throttle,
Spittle of grit
Grueling the headlong lips.

Machines come out of the moon,
Shocking the air back, sleek wind
At the speed of death.
Jabu says:
I will show you fear
In a handful of shit,
Flux and fettle
The robes close over.

And Jabu screaming, screaming
That God is Great.

Pharaohs and idols and the black stone
Fail in the dunes. The stars tremble
When the tracers rise, race over
A man stuck in the riddle,
Harum-scarum of a mind
Hung up in its own burnoose.

Out of the grind and clobber
Of the palm blades, the camels
Amok in the wadi mud,
Jabu says:
Lift me out of here
Like dew through a loophole,
And I will kiss
The elbows of the Almighty,
And steep the east
In these kneeling tears.

And Jabu screaming, screaming
That God is Great,

As the night dries, as the sun burns up
The air, the earth, the scream.

In the Offing

Sag wie lang wir gestorben sind

—Georg Trakl

It was the time of pigeons
Bottom-feeding on the plinth of the overcast statue,
One bronze arm broken off and pointing
Downward to the mass graves, imperial finger
Stirring the bones in the limelight.

I pick my way through the rubble of dusk,
Horizon brought low
As sugar in the blood. Even the flophouse fleas
Go down on their luck and knuckles,
Nosing a soft recess to die in.

These months, in the quiet moments,
Ideas of virtue visit me.
But they don't stay.
Evading the hard looks, they
Sidle their glances elsewhere, no more

Than spayed wisdom, the accidents of truth
One breaks through to
In the folds of fortune cookies,
Brittle and blandly aslant—
The smile of Buddha in a bad translation.

On a bare rack I crease my coat
Like a flag over a coffin. Night,
That stale apostle of the apocalypse,
Tucks me under its cold sheet, lays me
Deep in this dream—

Hot little combo at the *bal musette;*
Kiss-curls swishing the snapbrim caps;

Some warm woman under me,
Her small breasts sloping
Halfway down the ribcage like afterthoughts.

Outside, in the city, searchlights
Prod the black windows, rousing
The arts and the rats,
Making the barefoot assassin
Pause one beat in the hushed house,

Sweeping from pram to dish antenna, from ruins to
An all-weather madonna in the side yard,
Hard by the sticks
Of mongrel roses, her blue mantle chipped,
Crown the color of Chinese babies.

And what should we wake to?
Sleep is my hairdresser; dew, my ablution.
Hunger drew these dark circles under my eyes
And pinched a red stain in the stubble.
Though the winter chickadees

Grease their beaks with suet, and dogs
Breakfast on the gutter sops,
For us there's only
A fist in the midriff, meat on the run,
And figments offing the flesh of facts.

White Socks and Polkas

Is there no music to equal
The wheeze of a squeezebox in Cleveland,
A sound so crude and sweet
It's like a nun farting through novena?

And holding up the backbeat
There's always a snare and a bull fiddle,
With a saxophone out front
Honking down a three-step filigree.

I've put my time in, passed up
The punch tureen and turned to
The boys who hide a hard bottle
By the dark door of the Legion Post,

Their dim loud laughter raking
The old folks, the old country,
As they stroke the new hairs rising
Under their open shirts, their disco lavalieres.

Oh I've pressed their mothers
Close in my arms, hairdos so spray-straight
You couldn't budge them with a ballpeen hammer,
Slacks strung snug across their bellies

Until the stretchmarks strained in high relief.
I remember once a lowheeled woman who
Searched my body with her breasts
Like headlights on a lost highway

And whispered in my ear,
See that hag dancing? They must have
Thrown the baby back and kept the afterbirth.
Her eyes bore down like wet diamonds.

And the men too took me up,
Mouths rolling over dime cigars,
Jacking high the rafters with another round
Of leg-shaking sad-faced refrains.

They knew the stories I came to hear,
These heroes of the hardware bins,
Refugees from the packing plants,
Lying sidelong about love and money.

And always, before the night tied
Knots in their tongues, they felt the shock
Of their youth laid open, sobbing once more
For black bread and cabbage, for themselves.

I'm on a jag too, an outside echo
Of smoke rings and sweat
Freely seeping from a powdered brow,
Tribal rhythms that slide off the map—

A weather chart that says we're all as cold
And homeless as the rain.
And there's no curing this hangover,
Nothing that will heal the heart's harangue.

Sunday Social

Wet spring in Chapel Hill, and the hallways
Of the Carolina Inn are ringing with
The belles of Kappa Kappa Gamma,
Claptrap clappers of their tongues
Undoing the do's, the stacked lacquer, rattling
The calm and the Sunday silverware
At the Presbyterian Pre-Easter Lunch,
Pie-eyed grace before gravy. No one
Is looking for Diogenes under the dogwoods;
Plato has caved in, another pale shade
Among the purple shadows of wisteria.
These sisters of chiffon and the cotton vowels,
Ex-presidents of the Prom Committee,
Whose nipples rise like dunce caps
Under the pink delirium of their dresses,
Press a small smile in the lips, practice
The pig-soprano and the dripdry kiss, until
They've got it down cold. Outside,
On the damp verandah, Socrates is stirring
His hemlock on the rocks; Heraclitus
Steps in the same muddy puddle
Again and again and again. The ancient advisors,
Thin hands fatted with diamonds,
Powder the gin-rose from their cheeks,
Name tags spiked tight across the breast—
Mirabella, Sue Bob, June, and Orfamay.
But the noonday demon still sleeps, and the gods
Have already checked out, packing
Their wrath and their baggage. All over the South,
Something seems to be moving
In the kudzu and the flowering crab,
A breeze that sweetens the rainy air,
That brings to these pinched-in nostrils
The clove aroma of a downhome ham.

Far North of Ponchatoula

Lurleen's washing the cat, all right,
Foam-flares in the basement
And angry fur. I don't known where
The others went, this hard autumn,
Long after we had seen
The trees letting their green go,
A spree of leaves like a millionaire
Spending down his taxes. Could be
Junior's pitched out in the barn, watching
The geese congeal; could be
Ralph and Loretta have taken
Some remote road home, atlas
Cracked flat on the seat, their dark
Compulsions at the wheel. I've just come
Back from that bleeding dream, the old one,
With a hand scissored at the wrist
And reaching out to me. When I look
Beyond the windows, late and alone,
Twilight the color of cold oatmeal,
Nothing bends before me
But these trees, the hibernating trees;
And I can see how love comes close to
The accidental symmetries of fall,
Branches entangled by the wind, convulsing
The concave and the convex,
Like bodies doubled in distorting glass.

Color Photographs of the Ruins

*Plus belle que la beauté
est la ruine de la beauté.*

1

Even at this distance, twilight idling
In the background and the angle all wrong,
You can almost
Smell a panic of perfume
Circling her throat, and see
The startled ruckus of her hair
Like six flamingoes spliced to the skull.

And downwind from the dung and god-rot,
Her husband, his face like a dog
That's just barked up its dinner,
Looks out into the purples of elsewhere. He knows
That nothing lasting will ever last.

But she leans on ruin, on the scaling stone,
Her long arm locked over
A dragon's neck, as if no beast
Would ever best her, this woman who could
Stare down a rose, unmoving eye to eye.

2

Bent low behind his camera
Where the dust motes skim and flinch,
Alive in the light, in the summer solstice
He has travelled so far to find,
The star-scholar does not see them

As sequins of the sun, the young sun
Born through the seven red eccentric
Slots of the tower, whose sleeping secrets
Wait on his waking touch.

Over the broken sills,
The rays reach round him
Into the room, day making on the dirt floor
A perfect circle in the center,
The ancient golden shape of
Sorcery or calendars or savage worship.

And the dawn globes down, enclosing
The space that spans him, a white-annihilated
Sanctum of the sun, beyond defining,
For nothing can be known
Without limits, the landmarks of darkness
That compose enabling harmonies. And the dust,
Stirring from his footsteps as he

Stands here, shifts there, adjusting the shutter,
Will rise and blur and fall, filming
The black box he brought
To witness and to quiz
This air that dazzles, this lavishing light.

3

Cooler than noon, their spools advancing
To the next frame, they bribe the guide
Three times, silver deep in a brown palm;
In the slow dark they step down,
Three circles of descent

Under groin and cracked column, a burl
Of fat wood thrust out before them,
Pitch licking into pitch, until
They stoop through the last chamber, young
And still testing their flesh
In a wedding of doubt and desire,
The air now on them like a dead hand.

By the false tongue of the torch
And its yellow teeth, they take in
Those walls that echo to the eye, a sudden language
Centuries beyond them and still speaking,
Picked out in postures they understand,
Dim carvings and crude, craving
The body before the soul seeped in.

She feels the flame-rub, flame-spurt,
The worn glow over the stones; and he
Relives the first flash of hair, the secrets
Feared in the back pages his father hid:
Mouth manuals, aids to erection, unguents
And the oils of love. Breath born again
In labor, they find in each other's face
The promise left blindly behind; and know
This is what they paid for,
And will pay for, as the hired light
Sweeps far from them, scanning
The black raptures of a low relief.

A Late Theory of Reading

Drunk at midnight, head flat against
the open page of a book,
I can feel the words
crawl into my ear, insect syllables
that twitch the hairs of hearing
and climb the slow tunnel to the brain.

Something small and half-mad
crimps its thousand wrinkling legs
across my thought, looking for
a back way down to the tongue,
that slum of dreams and renunciation.
I don't move. Even the least breath
would break or drive astray
the crippled mystery of its passage.

Hymn and Harangue for Hesperus

In wry weather, when the air gives out
Exhalations of cold blood and ammonia,
And the entrails of the trees spell nothing,
Their trunks impaled against
The leafmeal spoilage of the north,

We turn to you, incautious star, Venus,
First cousin to the hanging judge
And the ellipse, keen kin of the edge,
Whose knifelight spikes through
The pearl and purples of early sleep.

Lady of the evening, unmoved by Palomar
Or milkrun jitneys to the moon,
Bend down to us, touch these mute midwestern
Disciples of the homely
With the dark hysterics of your tongue.

Others may come consoling you with poison murmurs,
Poor morsel, poor amazon,
Sick from kisses and the memorabilious rose.
But we live in your privilege,
Like that poet unashamed of his own sanity,

Fisheyed with awe, no longer bottlenecked by the blaze
And strict oblivion of gin—
That poet who repeats all night his thin lines,
Spliced and rudespun
And richer for all he has rejected.

Heliotropic

Notes from the provinces always start
With the weather

—Charles Wright

I've got my weather eye out
for the dog-eared azaleas and bitchwood, the cherries
lined up like an orchard of slot machines.

I'm in no mood for *Orphans of the North,*
undertaker's makeup on that silent
slyboots who leaps from floe to failure,

his true love set adrift by a villain
twitching the waxed whip-ends of his mustache,
while a slow cold front moves in.

Rack up that tape of *Beachball Libido,*
blankets squirming on the bedroom sand,
a surfbeat soundtrack as the sun barrels down

over breasts big as beerkegs, and the tanned young men
in shotpouch bikinis, muscles marinating in the heat,
lob and volley with their pinpoint heads.

Here it's a sky of overcast iron, the streets
iced down like a boxer's eye: *echt* Akron,
middleweight with the charm of a socket wrench

and a glass jaw nursing the count. I'm just
another groundhog hostage to the dark,
stooge stuck at the dead end of his trope,

waiting as this white on white gives way
to green inklings in the snow, catkins and squill
and all the spiky innuendoes of the spring.

Coroner

Cold mornings, he would warm his hands
In the steam clouding from a corpse
Wheeled in after love went bad
Three feet behind its skull. And then
Coffee, black and sweet, to keep down
The bile backed up from the night before.

With the chest hacked free and the organs
Slouched out like mutant amoebas, he would
Cradle the heart as if some pulse
Still pumped, his palms spread under
The valves slapped shut, the blood
Crawling through his knuckles to the steel groove.

And then the brain, that braided ball
Of sin and intuition, slides out on its own
Slick pulp, the stem ragged where the lead
Peeled back the core, the text, and left
A mind draining into darkness. How bright
The slab glares, white tiles and the tools sharp!

And if some chill breaks late through him,
It shudders out like sweat, as the body turns
Stubborn under his prying knife, the hard remains
A strata of earthtones, a rainbow of pain.
What secrets lie bare and split to the eye?
Snicker of scissors as the clock ticks down.

Proles Before Swans

When England, so long in the water,
Began to shrink, its fat tax-wrung aristocrats
Thinned out or packed across the Channel,
Gone down to Rouen with bankbooks blazing,
He turned from the spanner, from green tea
Drenched in a coronation cup, to a Lucky
Jutting from shut lips, fedora cocked low,
His trenchcoat open at a spywise flap,
Assassin of the aspidistra, back alley bane
Of the babu and the ringnose punk. Now
It's Veuve Cliquot with the mash and bangers,
An au pair girl on the public dole, breasts
Expeditious as Alps, her nights spent
Learning his tongue, her days rinsing his socks.
In the park, the starveling pondfowl
Nip at the nippers' gifts, bread and water
Enough to feather up the tour brochures.
Now it's boots and prattle in the bosky dark,
Alarms no laws will answer, the pedigrees
Lopped off and the ranks spread level: fishwives
Whiskeyed out at Wimbledon, a princess
Locomoting to a duckwalk guitar. And
In the higher reaches, the Minister for Home,
His stance the stiff carriage of a man
With a turd in his pocket, appeases
Whatever brings in the peace and pence:
Upholding the tasselled hems of jellabas, bribing
The priest-prone bombardiers, pledging his word
To the prescripts by which
All spite will be spayed, all slums annulled,
And palm trees planted on the stony shore
Of this island pickled in the brine,
Empire of pubs pouring out a headless brew.

February Lull

And so the sky says
—*Temporarily Out of Winter,*
After a day so cold
It made the manholes shrink,
And from the downtown streets
Drove home the sewer crews,
Blue police, and the crackheads
Bringing in the shivs—whiteout
Like a flurry of wild typists,
Only two snowflakes shy of a storm.

Okay by me, moans Alberta,
Girl with a big moosey name
And combustible breasts, her head
Sparking in the dark
At midlevel, each pull proving
The wave theory of light.

But some of you are still conducting
Postmortems of the thermostat,
Honing the flat shovels, putting an edge
On the steel studs. O city
Unaccustomed to anything but
The permanent torpors of twilight,

Don't waste one more weekend
On cable and the lazy paperbacks, or folksongs
Taking the pledge to public radio.
Hitch your red suspenders to the sun,
That sudden miracle, and join us—
We're all going down to the mall;
Will be back by ten.

Poem Written with the Eyes Closed

Black news on the doorstep at dawn
Can't shake my sleep; whatever the day's done now
To flesh and the future, I know that
No bell curve tolls for me. But your genius is
To build over those acres of moonlight
Where the alleys and coldwater flats become
The slums of milk and honey, erasing the night
Like a blackboard swept clean for the day's diagrams.

Who can live by those scruples
Of grammar and geometry? I take the dark
And move through it, coming to
Love by echo location, the bed
Always under a falling woman, unmade.
You call it blind luck or bones
Hot in a passing hand, but tonight
Your body is breaking all the laws of chance.

Film Noir

You're with a woman named Doreen—
Doreen of the leech lips,
Hat staked down to her head
With a stiff quill, Doreen who can
At the same time smoke and snap off
A wisecrack
Inflating the pink perfect
Circle of her chewing gum.

It might have been Chicago,
Or some place on
This planet . . .

Nightstreets greased with rain;
The shadow of a rat
Glistening on the garbage tins; drunks
And the lowdown lonely mopes
Looking for a lamp pole
Or a bandit—anything that's strong
Enough to hold them up.

You're packing heat, blue barrel
Cold against your heart, your hard jaw
Jacked up to a sneer
Striped sidewise where the light
Cuts through the slats to barber
The bristly stipples of a daydark beard.

And then a wheelsqueal at the corner,
Black sedan whose windows
Speak in tongues of flame,
A ratatat tattoo
Two feet above your ears, signals
Pricked in the brick wall,

And one wayward engraving
Deep in Doreen, against whose
Ballistic breasts you lay
The requiem of your grizzled cheek.

Brim of the damp fedora
At halfmast, leather sap sagging
On your thigh, you carry this grief
Like a big stick to the speakeasy,
One disarming eye in the peephole,
And then the grunt and the locks shot back—
Miasma of a sotweed sweat;
Fallen women with a pickmeup
And a *nom d'amour;* crankcase gin
Disinfected with a twist. Some hophound
Dreams on the bent keys, backed up
By the slow snares of jazz. You make it
A double, another, a sloppy third,
Shotglass sticky with the midnight mash,
Counterspin and remedy for love
And luck gone dead as a lady.

At the green baize, two aces up,
Between the hitmen and the fingersmiths,
Big Buster mops his brow, his neck
A ruff of fat, slumps of it
Flooding the suit, on his fingers
A mob of diamonds
Breaking the hardedged light
To flare and bevel, Havana
Nodding its head of ash.

In the bald glare of the game, you take
The seat prepared for you, and draw
Three weeping queens, a king
To keep as kicker in the toss.
And the chips fall, too many
For the center to hold, topless towers
Ruined and slouching towards bedlam.
And then a second heady crown
To crew your boat, and beat the bet.

When Big Buster turns his hand, behind him
Some moll with pointblank breasts
Massaging the heaps and humps that slide
Under the funeral sheen of his sharkskin,
The table stages a coronation
Stacked against you, a bastard royalty:
Three kings escorting his duple queens.

Too quick for anyone to sweep
The winnings in or crack a gat,
You leave three smoking holes
Inside his heart, your calling card,
And claim the money and the moll,
Jamming the door shut as you whisper
One word on the way out: *Doreen*.

Down the sour alley, a cat
Slicks its crippled fur against
A grifter whistling a threadbare tune.
You light a Lucky and slip it in
The red quiver of her lips.
When the moon leaks through,
The whole city seems dreamed up
By a juicer on the junk gazette.
Wind, as if from a ceiling fan,

Lifts the headlines from faces
Splayed on the sidewalk litter,
A steady stir of reeks and gleams.
You turn the collar of your coat
And hunch for home, the woman
Worming herself against you, her breath
Tense with promise and tobacco,
All the smalltime vernaculars of night.

Slow Classes at the Music School

There are some who never stir,
strumming all day
without strings, until the sounds come down
like intervals of angels, so pure
it is not possible to say
what sex they are, however hard one attends
to the dark recesses and attachments.

Others have let out from their instruments
the last ooze of air, inventing
a vacuum of bells, of valves compressed
so that the lips ache
to raise the tone of dead brass,
and the cheeks swell without release
in fat parodies of desire.

And there where silence licks its wounds,
some late romantic plays
apostrophes to steel, the strobe lights timing
his intuitions, as if his whole body
were wired to repulsive plugs,
the head held together with earflaps
snapped shut against the skull.

And here I am, one of the slow souls
stalled in this room, improvising
on an unknown theme that nerves itself beyond
the evidence, and trying to find
in these berserk scales a key by which
I can put my hands upon
the tonic resolution of a fatal accident.

Orpheus at the Orpheum

—for John Sokol

Whatever's doing on the moon tonight,
I'm down here, having passed
the moment of maximum anticipation
like a prom queen in a pickup truck.

Looking back (always looking back
at the black river that split my heart
in two, waters I still drag deep for love),
I know how the footlights of hell

that once turned my head around
now pay the rent. So it's come to this:
my high tunes hired out
to cool down the customers, dry ache

between the acts they rise to,
those boys whose breasts and weasel hips
grind and peel away the differences,
blue pangs in the rimshot light.

What do they care for Bach or Tennyson?
(Unlike Lord Alfred's aunt, they'd rather not be
clustered than cloven.) Their lives run only
on hormones and rumors and deathwish diets.

Tucked behind the wings, they tattle on
about the secret women of the world: Sasha
yammering under his yashmak, Mike's kimono
yanked up in a sumo squat. I'm tired of

moving through their catpurr puzzles,
privacies of silk: they're less than half
the half I burned behind me, too quick
to claim what wasn't mine to keep.

O let their lipsticks overlap
and straddle, leaving no room
for my tangled voice, my tongue
whacking these words until they lather. Backstage,

I raise a prayer for breakbone fever,
razors up the spleen—anything the gods might find
to silence me, who never could forgive
the men who done their mothers wrong.

And yet, after the hard dances smoke down,
I do my part, breathing back the bars
until the bottom of the song drops out
and my stricken syllables exhaust the joint.

For I was born stupid as a stone
no lyre could lift out of the dirt; no wonder now
my head floats open on a stream
of memory and near-misses, slow waves

that bear me up and break
in whispers on a lost shore:
Fool, fool, we care only
for the lucky certainties of life.

Coup de Théâtre

1.   Fast Mimes

The first one is climbing a rope, no it's a ladder propped
against the locked window of the woman he loves, no
it's pointed at the bedroom of the Lindbergh baby
who cries and cries without a sound. You can see him
scaling the invisible, rung after rung, faster and faster
until his hands blur and a hard wind rises from his
churning feet, a wind that blows back the hair of the
audience, bouffant and beehive and lank bangs. Three
more stand by the ladder to steady it, no they're slid-
ing down like submariners on a klaxon dive, hatched
for a new harrowing of hell. Down their white faces
drop dollops of sweat, a syrup too slow to appease
them—four mimes at full speed breaking the sound
barrier, their dumbstruck tongues stuck out.

2.   Grand Guignol Salami

Rope burns, splinters plucked from the hamper at the heel
of the guillotine, missed cues and nail parings, sighs
from the box seats—it all goes into the sausage, al-
ready twelve feet long and prehensile. Backstage, the
union crews are testing the slipknots, the blunt ends
that hold everything in, forbidden by their anti-cater-
ing-and-circumcision clause to slice or serve. If you
can't stand the grind, we tell them, get out of the
contract. Hung from the rear curtain like sash-
weights, the tubes cure in cigar smoke, wet stubs
abandoned by impresarios. Horrible, horrible, the old
charwoman mutters, another critic poking holes in
the performance, wringing her bloodmop for gravy.

3. Benefit Performance for Injured Magicians

After the blessing by nuns speedreading the rosary, by a
    rabbi's riff on the ram's horn, you listen to the rollcall
    of the missing: victims of levitation and card tricks,
    comely assistants strangled in a rainbow of scarves,
    merlins who disappeared up the shot silk of their
    sleeves. Already the stage is a barnyard of rabbit dis-
    bursements and the green squirt of doves, around
    which the dupes and volunteers step into locked
    trunks, the sawbox, the chambers of legerdemain. In
    the first rows slump the widows and orphans, dark
    crescents under their eyes like the smudge of crawl-
    ing dirt unearthed from a buried head. Behind them,
    the wizards of false floors and the fastfingered men,
    the women crossing their legs in spiderweb stock-
    ings, in heels so high they must balanced by a gyro-
    scope of sex. Down the red aisles of donation, ushers
    thrust out their top hats, and you reach deep behind
    your ears in memory of the injured and the aged:
    mind readers asleep on the blank side of the brain,
    escape artists lost in the self-embrace of their strait-
    jackets, conjure-men whose hocuspocus backfires
    from a crippled tongue. And then applause like the
    wingbeat of ravens, the whole show drowned in hy-
    draulics, the purging aspersion of tears.

4. Streetcorner Marionettes

Hemplines strung out from the knees and knuckles, the heel
    and neck, strands that vanish up the glassy stare of a
    skyscraper, that jerk and jitter in the unseen hands.
    All day it's Punch and Punch, the stiff angles of a
    dice tableau, the lucky polishing the razors in their

wingtips, the losers coming down like a gravity blade, making their point the hard way. All day it's dimes in the cool-cap, fedoras full of fives. Sundown around the burning barrels, they're taking a tokay cocktail from a paper sack, aperitif to the spoon and needle, the dreamdrunk smoke lacing their lungs. Whoever holds these lines has given them the twitch and fits, has put out the moon, that pale stooge, and the carbon exhaust of the stars. Now it's guerrilla misery and the nightstick dance. Look at them skew inside the low circle of the lamppost, from whose iron branch dangles the undue fruit of light.

Happily Ever Before and After

He makes the mirrors bulge. The fat man,
Mouser, pounce and paunch, loves
Nothing thin within him,

Hates the maxim that some minimum inside might
Need release, a rat gnawing through
The buffers on the bone.

You'll find it easy, the way to a fat man's heart,
That donkey engine, strain of steam in the clogged pipes,
Pressure building to a blow.

He's heaped in hard advice, relayed persuasions, as if
The virtues of half a loaf should starve him
Down to his small parts:

A morning bog of bran, noons of carrot marrow, fast nights,
And the melting sweat of exercise—full-figure skating,
The massive stroke of laps.

But in this globe, this womb expectant with itself,
The world's weight brought back to scale, he feels
No more sad than serene,

Keeping, like a bride's vow, the promise that flesh,
More or less, is fate, a pledge the will alone
Will not reduce.

Fat man, gorgeous at the groaning board, you can
Tell the grace cup from the coup de grâce.
Nothing takes you in.

After Listening to the Only Tape of the March 1956 Reading in Berkeley (Snyder, Whalen, McClure, Rexroth, Ginsberg)

—for Walter Lehrman

I could sit up all night
and gossip about the Absolute, the whole room
blazing like a Buddhist suicide as someone
passes the six-pack this way and the pretzels
twist inward while the five tongues unwind:
Rexroth nursing a rhyme over the coughs and catcalls
and Gary still won't come down from the backwoods, McClure
putting the crowd on snooze-control and Ginsberg taking
his new all-weather strophes out for a test drive and Whalen says
none of the women he loved could walk a straight line anyway.
I turn to the expert on Kerouac for the laying on
of secondhand footnotes to the life
that crossed you like boxcars sparking through Bolinas,
each year switching you onto the wrong track, the one
that carries pig iron and potash and three-ply tires,
the one that disappears forever down the icy flats of Ohio
as the tape wheels on through daybreak, transporting
these poems across state lines for immortal purposes
and leaving behind the voices, all spent jism and bad jazz
around the downbeat drumrolls of the blood.

At the James Wright Poetry Festival

Seven shades of green sprung loose
On the hills of Ohio, a May rain
Slicking down the strip mines
And the dogwoods coming back
Pink and white, open
Like a new set of false teeth.

We took the slow road, sinking
Through those river towns that float
Into each other, staking their limits
On buckshot signs in the fireweed.
They let their bad luck show, knowing
There's nothing on the far shore
But the hollows and humpback mills
Of West Virginia, that darker twin
Begot on the same worn mother.

And then the weekend streets
Of Martins Ferry, where its late native son
First saw and set down
The epic sadness of America,
A lifetime later looking up
From his poems to say:
After what I've written about this town,
I can never go back.

We walked his lines again:
The houses of old brick
Slavered with paint and half built over;
The sidewalk benches backed
With placards calling us
To the Hall of Improved Red Men,
One more powwow of bingo and burnt pig;
The dusk falling out on children

Who put by their balls and bikes
And stood inside the railed porches,
Waiting for something to change.

And at the podium, some poet
Imported for the praising
Welcomed the townsfolk by telling them
How, in Wright's incisive books,
Their wasted lives lay open on the page—
As if it were her privilege as a guest
To spit in the host's soup.

It was then we felt
His gravestone pounded into place again,
Sumac uprooting the raw soil.
It was then we felt
The endless backwash of the Ohio,
Bearing away the trash
We fill it with, lifting our ugliness
To another state, and bringing to these banks
Whatever has been heaved in
At its inhuman source—sick water
Born to purify itself
Only on those obstacles so hard and high
That this day must break before it passes.

A Riff for Isadora

*She knew the Greeks as well as an average girl from
the state of Ohio can know them.*

> —Zbigniew Herbert

You know the downside:
a braid of tendons, the red voice
reversing in alarm . . .

Maybe she had big feet
Maybe she would suck on the word *thalassa*
until the slipped skin
spilled purple from her lips
Maybe her soul floated
over the footlights, so high
she never saw that
even in the holy land of Russia
a loose tunic would leave
the farmboys sick and excited

One night she was
a lake shaken by the wind
One night she was
a goatskin of camel's milk
loped to butter on a woozy hump
One night she was
the deathlore of Brahms, the stars pushed back
by a swollen moon, the dark
equilibrium of rubies

Maybe that poet whose smoke
feathered her body in a Slavic bed
would whisper the sole line
passed down from Lord Alfred's brother:

After all, angels
are only a clumsy form of poultry.

O she was mean and golden,
lost in a low age the years have
washed over like a bar rag
on a sloppy drunk, the good wood
gleaming in the lamp's amber
and the tip tray graced with nothing
but the legends of replenishment,
ukuleles and a jeweler's loupe . . .

Confluences at San Francisco

—MLA, 1987

From the high line spun over us, we hang on to
The clang of cable cars
As the damp city drops downhill, steeped
In fog and the sharp ascension
Of a pyramid whose stones inter the soul
Of money, whose shadow falls across
The Marxist cash bar and the hiring stalls.

In the glass house of the Hilton, they're raising
The ghost of Derrida, they're plotting
The Empowerment of the Disembodied, in one hand
A cluster of bloody nuts, in the other
The secondhand theories—so many thin breasts
Supporting the beards and tweeds,
So many daring to be glib and equivocal!

In the unwindowed rooms, the voices summon up
A future banked behind the podiums,
As the past grinds its teeth into dust,
Into a dead tongue
That wags against the waste, the forced accounts,
The grievances so old and heavy
Even the bay's salt air can't bear them away.

Far from any session of sweet silent thought, we feel
The pressure crowd inside our heads
Like the giant hissing cockroach of Madagascar;
And suddenly remember that parakeet
Who pecked on marijuana seeds until he sang
A wobbly daylong obbligato to the cage—
One more small mind spent in its own making.

Missing Mayakovsky

Mayakovsky was and remains the best and most talented of our Soviet poets. Indifference to his memory and to his work is a crime.

—Stalin, 1935

Vlad the flywheel, Vlad the bayonet—

You would kick back the slush of Odessa,
As if your boots could unspring
The booby traps of truth. On either side,
A snowbank of skeletons with breasts,
Rats sucking the bony milk; and in the air,
A ghost of snow, beckoning,
The spirit of Esenin who split his wrists
And, with his own spoiled blood, wrote
A farewell poem, then hanged himself—
So you, too, have put down
An early elegy, staring into the white nights:
More and more often I think:
it might be far better for me
to punctuate my end with a bullet.

But after the spring and pangs
Of the revolution, how could you
Leave these women behind, abandon the anguish?

Lily, whose kiss you craved
To cauterize your lips; and Tatiana,
The swan arc of her throat, her heron eyes,
Exiled to Paris where you stood
All night at the gaming tables, losing,
Longing to lose yourself
Deep in her arms and then send the next morning
Another helpless telegram
To Lily, bitch of the distant shimmer,
Begging for her love. No wonder
You would wound yourself

With a shotglass of vodka, the peppercorns
Rolling at the bottom, their hot gleam
Black as ball bearings from hell.

No wonder you would laugh
When the world called out for poems
Soft as a doe dappled under summer boughs,
And you gave them your hard lines
Honed in the street, sharp in the heart—
O Baudelaire of the Soviet!
But you would have no truck with
Demotic rhapsodies to the tractor
And the ten-year plan, no inkhorn
Disemboguements on the page—
Only a spiked tongue, a turn
That let no eye escape
The soup kitchens, the dead souls, the birch
Bound back to earth by a chain of ice.

And when they plucked that bullet
From your skull, and lifted the brain
From its pan to the pantheon, a mile of mourners
Stalled by your body, the flowers teased
Into sickles and hammers and screws:
An iron wreath for an iron poet.
Five years later, they plugged your ashes
Near the graves of Gogol and Stalin's wife,
Building over those bone scraps
A monument to praise and keep you quiet
Under red tons of marble, under black,
Where even now, provoked by
The throes of its live desire,
Your dust bears up
The dead weight of the age.

Elegy with Sideburns

I've been keeping the Elvis deathwatch,
ten years tamped under
the downstream dirt of Memphis, pampered
by horseshoes of roses, nosegay guitars.

All the black records hiss and pitch,
a grave dug deep in the grooves—
O Panamas of pain, Suez of sex and menace!

I want to charter a night flight for Vegas,
change this channel with a .45! I want
to feel my head fill up
with fog awkward off the river, cancelling
the stars, the deadlines pressing on the century.

I want to pour this stillborn bourbon
down the throat of a dream, syntax strangled
in the spirit, a ghost that rolls away
its own stone and rocks the inexplicable.

And if that stub in the bottleneck
melts down the darkness, it'll be
too late for sleep, too soon for Jesus.
I'm holding the last great wake
before the day takes over, halfway between
the gospel bells and the gutbucket blues,

a backbeat steady as the rhythms of the sun.

Insomniacs at the Feet of Science

After the nightcaps, the thick history
Of hydroponics and the welfare state,
They put out the lamp,
Blue sheets bogged around them
Up to the peepholes, the hollow brow,
Until they're all mucked in
Like pigs in a drizzle.

Ah, what can the doctors do,
Locked on the false side of the mirror
Where the secondhand machines
Push out their bushwah, red eyes
Pulsing near the coma zone? Someone
Has lost a sponge in the Sleep-O-Meter.
Someone's scribbling a list of the new theories:

1. Windpipe attached to the eyelids;
2. Poetry and the examined life;
3. Romanian fears of the moon;
4. Bad enchiladas on the graveyard shift.

Perhaps the cure lies in something sucked through
The cable, some sitcom of crippled accountants;
Or something perhaps in lipstick and lingerie;
Or, better yet, a crowbar to the brain.

Perhaps, like the handsome milkman, the mousing cat,
They want only to delay the day, the sun
That severs us from everything
Warm and dark and unresolved; waiting
To be born again from hibernation
And the mother tongue, the mysteries
That lick us slowly into shape.

Ego Scriptor

Another day of dorsals circling the boat. . . .

I am thinking of the golden vowels of Christ,
Italicized, and of Hamlet,
Whose mind is mutiny, a cocked hawk
With the legs of a ballet master.

Some have said to me:
Rogue scholar, pull down your cowl.
You could not quiver
The membrane of an idea, nor would wisdom
Leave on your lips
The errant residue of a kiss.

But I have seen the stockings stop
At the black grin of a groin,
And have not, like Ruskin,
Come undone, limp
With horror at the dripping hair.

What is the point
Of entry? Night takes everything
Out of us like a stomach pump.

Those who pray to
The gods of novocain, the gods
Who ease our sleep with
A consolation of blades, know
That something troubles the waters—
A dragline moon or slipway of oil,
Wavebreaks flinched with fins. . . .

Some have said of me:
He is not a man for landscape.
The supple valleys, peak, and plain,
Mean no more to him
Than the glass glare of a mall
Smeared with eager faces stroking their hunger
For the broken bread, the wine-dark wine,
Stained by the seizures of restraint.

But I have stood beneath
The ancient arthritic oaks, propped up
On their rough crutches, and watched
The way a tree gives with the weather,
The way the rattailed clouds
Rasp the heavens clean.

So what if the wind talks back,
A riposte from the grave? Night re-
Hearses the held breath, the pulse
Stalled on the offbeat.

Even in the shallows, the oars sweep in
Pinked with teeth. . . .
The only bridge I can build
Stands by
The handsaw carpentry of words.

I put down what I put down,
Plug all the vents
From kitsch to cabala, break
The plate tectonics of the brain.

It's time. Get out
The do-rag and the bucket, the suckling
Solace of a cigarette, and mop up
The pity drizzling from these dolls that bleed.

I am dreaming of Li Po drunk in the moon,
His body seeking its own level,
Deep and done, the poems dropped overboard,
Drifting like Ophelia, faceup, whose heart
Was wooed by water, whose voice,

Buoyant on the undersurge, unfathomed,
Floated for the slow receding shore.

Interrogation of the Usual Suspect

What passes for the truth
passed through these lips,

weaselly, strange, with a wild
staccato of the hands, the head

sidling and sinking like a heavyweight
whose only hope is

the bell or a bought judge.
Where were you when? And who

will swear on his mother's daisied grave
to your saintliness, or at least

a whorelong weekend pissed away in gin?
Lacking the cancelled stub, the spinster witness,

you fend off the jokes, the java,
the cop who has at heart

your cleared release, the words reeled in
round and round a dizzy spool—

as you would, in braver years, ride out
a boot abrupt to the bowels,

epiphany of spittle in the bloody teeth.
And if the alias, the alibis

break down, driven backward
by their files or your quisling fingerprints,

you must hold fast and lie,
bring to this rinsing sweat

the stain of sticky answers,
and let them prove

what you and they both know,
how guilt reclaims an early innocence

for all the noose that fits.
Outside the echoes of confession,

their only recourse is
to court you, until they hear

the last black rap
of the gavel, a hard fall

sealing what the mouth admits,
or setting free the stringent tongue.

Straight, No Chaser

At the thin end of Main Street, even the Alibi Lounge
Has barred its doors to heartbreak, has had it with
The shotglass lies of love; even the rats
Have packed their bags for a dragtail return
To the House of Vermin, the Mildew Hotel.
That man abandoned on the sidewalk could be
Sucking up to the moon, with an air of traveler's Italian
That limps through the night, its rhythm sprung as a dead bed,
Pain eking out the misplaced glamour of negation.
Though his song comes begging against the dark windows,
There'll be no music in this house but Thelonious Monk.

Plato of the black keys, deconstructing the standards
With X-ray theorems of the inner theme, you deny
The sacked attachments, romance wrung out and racked
Like a saxophone bitching around the bottom of a tune.
You deny the cotton deprivations of brogan and overhauls,
Straw hat unraveling at the edge; you deny
The double-clutched inertia warmed up by dreamlight in the vein.
Even the blood marriage of bones and the gospel tambourine
Can't overcome the moans of the middle passage.
Angular velocities, forearm stomping down the ringfinger trill—
There'll be no music in this house but Thelonious Monk.

In this house we'll have nothing but the music of the Sphere—
No deathmarch metronomes, bull fiddle slapped in the head;
No seasick guitars or the bronze concussion of cymbals.
Let the geek and the gunsel stand dripping under
The fishy reek of rain; let the shadows writhe with women,
Whispers and mysteries of their lifting skirts.
How we all want to confess, come clear about
Our sulphur indiscretions, black purge and pledge,
Mongrels lapping after the oily emoluments of love.
But the blues blare back, glare of a cyclops in the horn's bell,
Big baby brooding on the world, and only one eye to weep with.

From the Book of Original Entry

Those who can still hear the snap
Of their hatchback dreamsuits, or keep
Bronzed and lopeared on their desks
Memento mori of the bunny slippers,
Stretch their brows across the past

To the hinterlands of infant calamity
(Thumbs unplugged; breasts so talcum-fat
The tongues lapped into powdered milk),
All the busy backward years that leave them
Looped with a sundown bourbon, spilling out

Rotgut impromptus on the spring
(Tulips adroop; the catkin branches
Bringing up a nursery of plumes and peeps),
Odes hatched from a broken heart; while others,
No early hurt to hound them or prod a howl,

Sing uncertain of their source: the glassbelled
Muse of museums; or that daemon whose eyeballs
Touch the world like skinstripped fingertips; or a clerk
Hunched late at his heavy ledger, counting the costs,
Who knows that even doggedness deserves its bone.

Ditch Lilies

Somewhere south of that blacktopped hour
where the citronella fails
on the patio, out past the cornpone boutiques
and the racket of chicken trucks
in a red squall of feathers, this road

lets out all its misery, so much nearer home.
And in the traffic's afterlight, one sad turtle
spins by me on its rim like a hubcap snapped loose,
my heart so raced up
no radar gun could clock its revolutions.

Fishhead music on the dashboard, clatter of cattails
and lilies in the ditch—
and the sudden headbeams run her down, misspelled sign
held out, hair in a swoon, face sucked in
as if her last good meal came back bitter to the tongue.

Out of the highway dirt, downdrag of the sun
where night fattens like a swampleech,
I take her in, crone shoes and croker sack; and she tells me
how her right eye slips out of reach,
sullen in its manners, and how the prayer flags of Tibet

give up their words to wind and weather,
to gods of the steaming yak. She gnaws over
the old soupbones of love and money,
hot sauce on the cold muslin, shotgun divorce—
all those hair triggers trembling at the oil of a fingertip.

And somewhere north of the state line, under stars
stopped in their tracks, I turn her
back to the gravel, where the nearby fields
stand stuffed with enough cotton
to keep their side of the conversation up till dawn.

All right, she says, the door slammed so hard
every window wavers on the world,
Don't let the moon fumble this one. But I do,
driving the wrong dark way for miles,
another summer sidewise on the wheels of amnesia.

Sepulchritude

When death, its fingers still strong with
tobacco and the secret hair of women,
opens at your throat
a blade poised
to pare back all indecision from the bone,

it will be too late for patient argument
or pleas against the dark, too hard
to bargain with your tongue
crouched low in the jaw,
your eyes evicting everything they see:

dry sockets; dyslexia of the grotesque. And yet
some sick attraction pulls you to
this seedy end—a sharp
influx of breath,
the heart strangling as it did in mid-October

when the moon cut through a wake of clouds
and the black streets crackled with
a static of leaves,
your voice lost
in the fall, in a red gust garbling the air.

Revelation: The Movie

I'd give it five stars,
if there were any left, so many having
flamed out in the firmament.
This flick's a cross between
Apocalypse Now and the leather resurrections
of some S & M cock-opera called
Bound to Come. You'll know the hero
by his dropdead looks, his sword of hairy righteousness,
his big bazooka for the jezebels:
he puts the *mess* back in *Messiah.*
But it's more than just
another pic of pecs and peckers;
this hardball boxoffice-buster has it all—

toads and hailstones, locusts gunning in
like a motorcycle gang, bad grammar in the overbite;
a woman with eagle wings, her hair the color of
gold tried in the fire of a bottomless pit;
candles and sandals and rods of iron;
an angel with a chain, and four more
cornered up the back alleys of the earth,
and seven angels hellbent on mayhem, and in the crowd scenes
a cram of angels, a mob, a ring, a rout—
O angels up the wazoo! And odors and ointments,
fornications on the wormwood waterbed; a soundtrack
flat-out into hyperdrive, warp of the turbo tubas,
red smears from the trumpet, flimflam on the drum;
and blood strangling out of the winepress; dragons in heat;
machine-edge of the Oscar-copping lines; beasts
with more heads than a college of liberal arts,
each one expelling a brimstone breath;
and dogs and sorcerers and whores; and a choir
goosed up in its robes and haloes, like a dago pope on cocaine,
warbling of Armageddon and the man.

I wish I had ten points locked in on the net;
I wish I had the in-flight option,
earphone rentals on the nonstop routes; I wish I had
half the popcorn handle, gnawed and scorched.
This baby will break out
in every burg on earth, no bargains at the matinee,
no passes, no refunds, full fare in the balcony,
and the promos dragging them in—the spuds
and the mall zombies, cornwise heifers from the heartland,
downtown jailbait on the make, the high and the Holy Rollers—
they'll all freeze in their seats, eyeballs wired
from the teaser to *The End,* each pair scanning for
the flash of a name and a new address, as the credits
crawl up the dark drop of the afterlife.

Exploded View of the Universe

I never wanted to
hang out with the godhead, all those cherubs
abeam on a nimbus, little fat faces winged
and smiling a million miles an hour
like a TV evangelist confessing the sins of his rivals
and quoting from the *Book of Solvency,* chapter eleven,
a verse undisturbed since the twelve tribes
wept and bitched and brought down from the mountain
their stone tablets cracked at the core:
Woe unto they who hoardeth gold away from me,
For it profits a man not. Nor did I
envy the French, those scholars of the rabble
and the absolute, who lost their heads
over the Enlightenment, finding in the mind alone
a cure for queens prinked out
in the low drag of milkmaids, a leveling of
the Latin elevations of wheat and wine—
their cobbled brilliance heaped up
like barricades against the darker truths.

I would split this life down the middle
and step inside, as happy to lie back
with the whalebone buttons undone, smoking
a two-foot cigar in an igloo, as to study
the meanings of the moon, all love a jade
where the willows lip at the river.
Let there be squabbling in the dovecotes,
classrooms berserk with children
addled by sex and mathematics: I will bring them
the brass loneliness of bells, the enigma of pretzels
packed in a broken lunch; I will bring them
scents and premonitions of a clumsy spring.

Somewhere inside myself, I am holding in each hand
the end of a wire stretched taut for the twang
of thin music, a tightrope for the soul
to stroll upon like a tired sparrow
gripping the crosstalk of a windblown line—
each step balanced by a vaulter's pole, prepared
this time to fall higher and higher, rising
through the amnesties of earth and air.

About the Author

Born in 1945 in New Orleans, and raised in nearby Slidell, Louisiana, ELTON GLASER graduated from the University of New Orleans (B.A. 1967; M.A. 1969) and the University of California, Irvine (M.F.A. 1972). His first book of poems, *Relics*, was published in 1984, and his second collection, *Tropical Depressions*, won the 1987 Iowa Poetry Prize. Other awards include fellowships in poetry from the National Endowment for the Arts and the Ohio Arts Council. Glaser is Professor of English at the University of Akron.

Pitt Poetry Series

Ed Ochester, General Editor